There was a snowman competition in the newspaper.

Gromit wanted to win the competition, so he made a snowman.

It was very good!

3

Wallace wanted to win the competition too. He had a new invention, the Snowman-o-tron! It made snowmen.

Wallace began to drive the Snowman-o-tron back.

Oh no!

Gromit stood in front of his snowman to stop the Snowman-o-tron bumping into it.

The Snowman-o-tron stopped.

Here we go, Gromit. I will show you how to make a snowman.

The door of the Snowman-o-tron hit Gromit's snowman.

Smash!

Then a snowman came out of the Snowman-o-tron.

It was not very good!

Gromit was not very happy.

He went back into the house and shut the door with a bang.

Bang!

The snow fell off the roof of the house …

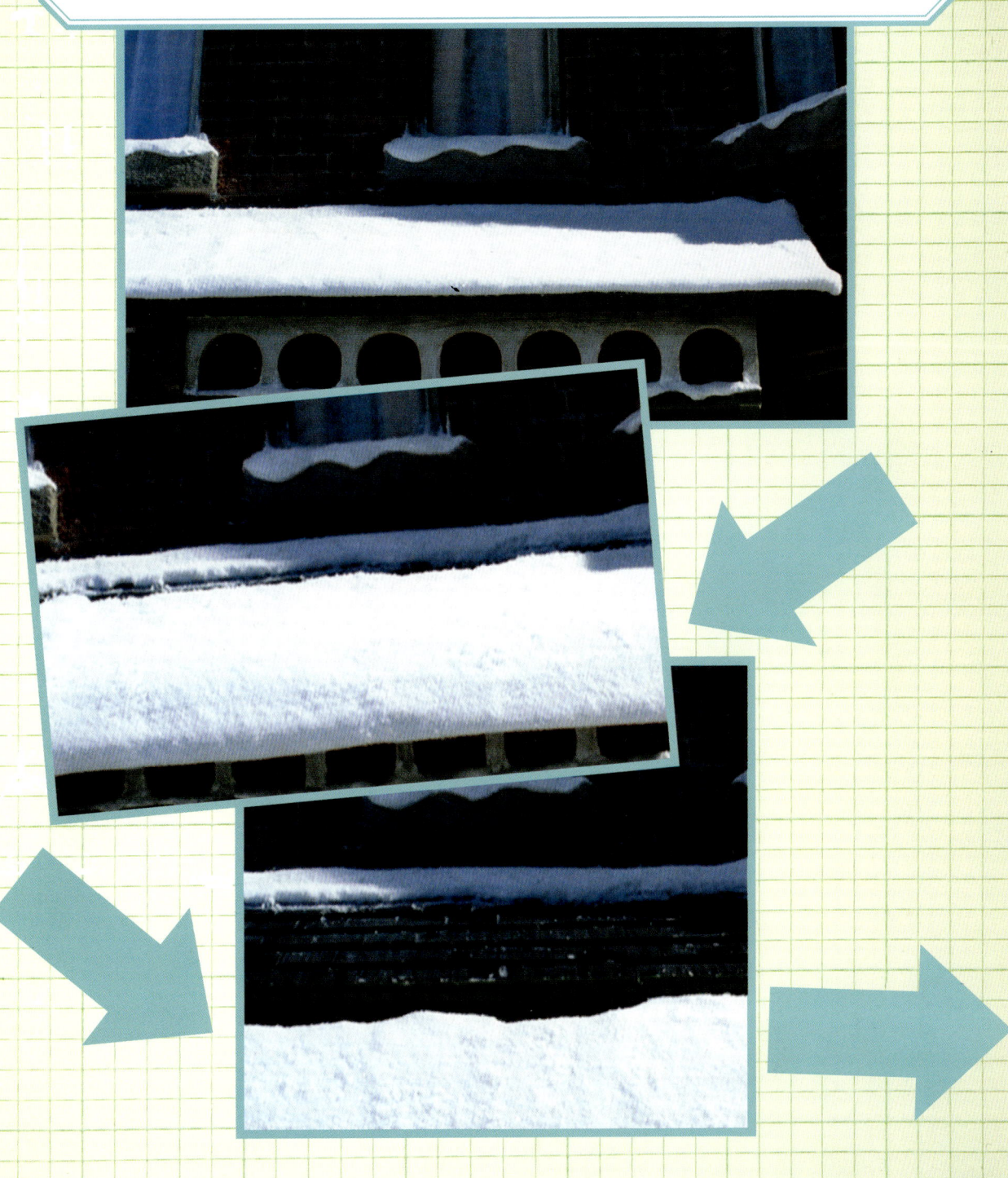

... right on top of Wallace!

Oops!

Gromit put some eyes and a nose on Wallace.

Now he had a snowman for the competition!

Gromit won the snowman competition. His photo was in the newspaper.

Gromit won a **big, gold** cup.

Wallace did not get a big, gold cup. But he did get a cold!

Aaachoooo!